This book presents an empowering and theoretically sound framework for understanding and correcting what is keeping you from doing your best in business, sports, and life. *High Performance Thinking* (1) helps you identify your default settings for responding to performance situations; (2) teaches you how to analyze the quality of those responses; and (3) discusses ways to improve those that are less productive than you want them to be. These concepts, tools, and techniques are presented in a straightforward style that is filled with wisdom, wit, and experience.

high performance thinking

FOR BUSINESS, SPORTS, and LIFE

Gayle A. Davis, Ph.D.

Psychology Connections
Colorado Springs, Colorado

First printing.

Psychology Connections, Dr. Gayle Davis, 730 West Cheyenne
Boulevard, Colorado Springs, CO 80906, 719-632-5761
www.GayleADavisPhD.com

Book design by Dorie McClelland, Spring Type & Design

Publisher's Cataloging-in-Publication
(Provided by Quality Books, Inc.)

Davis, Gayle A.
    High performance thinking for business, sports and
life / by Gayle A. Davis — 1st ed.
    p.cm.

    1. Self-management (Psychology) 2. Self-help
techniques 3. Success   I. Title.

BF632.D38 1999   158.1
                               QB199-750

ISBN 0-9672835-0-7

to
John

Contents

Preface

In the twenty years that I've been working in sports psychology, the field has undergone a major transformation. The current acceptance of sports psychology is a welcome change from the early days when it was considered a questionable, perhaps frivolous, waste of an athlete's time. Sports psychology today has become an accepted, even expected, aspect of preparation for competition in amateur and professional athletics alike. Indeed, *USA Today* states that sports psychology— learning how to think and behave in ways that enhance one's physical skill—is "being heralded by athletes as the performance revolution of the 1990s." [August 1996]

My involvement in sports psychology is the result of my enthusiasm for figure skating, and my desire to add variety to a busy professional life while I continued to provide a service and benefit to others. This part of my practice grew rapidly and I began working with athletes from a wide variety of sport disciplines. These athletes possess varying levels of expertise, from backyard amateurs to World and Olympic contenders. I also work with coaches from many parts of the world.

I quickly realized that what was good for a sport was also good for other aspects of life. Everything I found to be true for enhancing an athlete's performance, I found to be true for enhancing performance in any area of life. More and more, while working with people who sought more successful performances, I found myself using sports psychology strategies.

The term sports psychology is a synthesis of theory and practical experience. It consists of psychological discipline together with proven principles and techniques. Combined with a person's physical skills, sports psychology can enhance practice and performance, regardless of age or skill level. Though designed for athletes preparing for competition, these techniques for personal improvement can be readily applied to any aspect of life by anyone who recognizes a need and has a desire for self-improvement.

A variety of these techniques can be identified and applied to enhance performance and increase success. The key is that what we think is as important as what we do. By consistently combining mental skills with physical skills, anyone can improve their performance, whether that performance is at a board meeting or on the playing field, at the PTA or the PGA.

Most of us had the children's story, *The Little Engine That Could,* read to us many times. That story is about a little engine that needed to tell itself over and over, "I think I can, I think I can, I think I can," while attempting to do something that it had previously felt it could not possibly do. Its goal was accomplished through desire and successful thinking and is a wonderful story about mind over matter.

Another great example is from nature. Most know that a bumblebee cannot fly. We understand that there is much scientific evidence supporting this. His body is too heavy; his wings too light. Aerodynamically, it is impossible for the bumblebee to fly, but fly he does.

How does sports psychology translate to other areas of life? Most people can relate to the struggles and successes of athletes. While athletes have a specific practice routine and lifestyle to enhance their innate talents, they also deal with the same issues and concerns that all of us do. They have fears and expectations that come into play beyond the training and discipline of their sport. They set goals, experience setbacks, respond to change, and continue to refine their picture of themselves. So, the transition from sports to other areas of life is easy.

The belief that mental skills can measurably add to a person's performance is the premise of this book. You may have read numerous publications that conveyed this concept, yet still not have a true understanding of how to use sports psychology techniques to your benefit. *High Performance Thinking* will guide your understanding and application of the principles of sports psychology for business, sports, and life. If you are interested in evaluating and improving your performance in any area of your life, this book is for you.

1

◆

Introduction

Thinking is critical to everyone. To know just how critical is to understand that our mind works using talk and pictures, and that the content of our internal dialogue and visualizations determine how we proceed through life.

If you are not getting what you want out of life, go into your mind to understand why and what you can do about it. You have old settings that were put there by others. They are your personal collection of experiences, thoughts, habits, and memories. Your personal input is never rooted permanently, but rather is fluid and can be changed. With effort, these settings can be modified, enhanced, re-learned. As adults, we have control over how these old settings influence us.

When I started working with skaters, I realized that most figure skaters practice 1,000 or more hours a year (60,000+ minutes) and yet might compete for only twenty minutes during that same year. When we think about competing for such a short time, we want the athlete to make those twenty minutes as productive as possible. Her technical skills have already been put in place. She is well-trained, nutritionally sound, and has a good energy level. What may be missing is her confidence or her ability to understand and use her mental skills for more successful performances. She needs to know that the greatest resource that any athlete brings to competition is their mind.

So much of what we do is considered mental. Some experts say that as much as 95% of our performance is mental after we have skill development. This means that having the technical skills is one thing, and vitally important, but being able to actually perform our skill under pressure and when necessary is what really counts.

We all have a mental picture of who we are, who we want to be, and how we want to be. The closer we are to that picture the happier we are. The farther away, the less happy. If the difference between your mental picture and what you are doing is great, you need to determine what is creating the difference—the picture itself or the actions you are selecting to achieve the picture. You might have an unrealistic picture. Or, without realizing it clearly, you might be performing so that your picture will not be achieved. Or, something in your subconscious might not really want you to match your picture. Whatever is creating the difference, you need to bring reality and your picture closer together. This will mean adjusting your picture or adjusting your performance by thinking differently.

It is useful to evaluate your picture of yourself to see if you are measuring yourself against someone else's yardstick or expectations, or if you put yourself up against others who are at more advanced skill levels. Common sense tells us that this is self-defeating, but it is easy and common to fall into measuring oneself by inappropriate yardsticks.

Why do you act the way you do? Through the years, everything that anyone has ever said or done to you has shaped what you believe and how you perceive the world. From that you formed a mental picture of yourself and, true or not, that is what you base your feelings and behavior on. When you think, "I can't do it," who's telling you that? A parent? An influential person from early in your life?

If you are not where you want to be, you are still using that original input; and the resulting behavior just isn't working. The subconscious mind is just like a computer—it takes what you put in; it doesn't question; it takes input as fact and gives it back. If you tell yourself one thing enough times, or you hear something enough times, you create a habit or belief. At any point in time, you are either doing better than you thought, or not as well as you think you should. You are always somewhere on that continuum.

In *High Performance Thinking,* we will first explore the mind and how it works and discuss the importance of self-talk and visualization. Then, we will examine a model of behavior that isolates some specific mental skills and looks at each of them to see what they consist of and how they are used. Finally, we will show how to use these skills in a practical way to increase or enhance performance in any area of life.

By reading this book, then learning and practicing appropriate mental skills, the correct information will be in place when your mind goes to the past in search of the resources you need to achieve your goals.

We're in charge of our minds. We weren't involved in forming the original input but, today, we can change our information through self-talk and visualization. The subconscious is a vast reservoir of resources and information. Our task is to identify what is in its recesses, determine whether that information is helpful or hurtful, become aware of how it affects our performance, and use constructive mental techniques to block it or improve it. The result is instead of using responses and thoughts from earlier years, we think, feel, and do based on beliefs and ideas that work for us today.

2

◆

The mind and how it works

Specific mental skills are proven important to create successful outcomes. High performance athletes use these techniques to enhance performance. Have you ever observed highly successful athletes and wondered how they have perfected their performance to the level that they have? I'll take you inside and show you the mental skills they have developed. I will identify those mental skills so you can duplicate them in your life. To do so first requires that you understand how the mind works.

Imagine your mind as a very long hallway. At one end is a window with light coming in. As far back as that light goes—about 20%—is the conscious part of your mind. You are in your conscious mind when you are alert; you are aware of sounds and light; you are communicating, acting, and being. If you continue down the hallway, the light gets dimmer and dimmer and, finally, becomes pitch black. Now you are in the subconscious—the remaining 80% of your mind. Everything you have ever heard, read, felt, seen, or said to yourself throughout your lifetime is stored here. Imagine that on either side of the hallway are filing cabinets from floor to ceiling containing this information.

Some of those filing cabinets contain the mental skills that elite and successful athletes use. The information within those mental skill files creates a way of responding that makes them feel, think, and behave as they do. Just as athletes find it necessary to become aware of what is in those particular cabinets and adjust them accordingly, so should you.

The filing cabinets are largely made up of input from childhood when the information was literally poured into you without conscious reflection or choice on your part. Your experiences have caused you to modify some of your response patterns; but, unlike the high performance athlete, you may not have made that a concerted, conscious effort. Therefore, you would not get the same high performance results.

Athletes understand that their performance skills come from these "filing cabinets," and that the way they feel, communicate, and manage their time in relation to their sport comes from there. This works in the following way. A skater goes down the ice and prepares to do a double axle. As she is going down the ice, her body consciously gets into a certain position in response to a message from the conscious to the subconscious that she wants to do a double axle. Her subconscious locates her double axle filing cabinet and instantly her body responds by getting her feet in the correct position to execute the jump. In the file is a blueprint of the way she does the double axle. The blueprint may be correct or incorrect, but her body will follow that blueprint unless she makes some conscious adjustment. Therefore, if she usually finds herself going down the ice, effectively executing the entry but rotating short of

9

the desired revolutions and then landing, that is what she will do. If the blueprint shows her consistently landing the double axle while doing the correct number of revolutions, she will do that. With no intervention, the mind and the body have no choice but to follow the blueprint.

Another way to think about this is that the instant the conscious mind tells the subconscious that the skater is ready to do a double axle, a tape recorder plays the sequential steps that she has done repeatedly to form a habitual response. This process can work in her favor, and often does; or it can work against her. So, if she doesn't like the blueprint or habitual response pattern, she needs to first become aware of what's wrong, what needs to be fixed, then learn how to fix it.

Another important thing to understand about the mind is that you can only think of one thing at a time. It often seems that you are, indeed, thinking of more than one thing; but, because the thoughts are coming in such rapid-fire succession, it only seems so. Imagine that your mind is like the "thought cloud" above a person's head in a comic strip. And that only one thought can be represented at a time. Only when that thought moves out and clears the space can another thought enter that same space. Or, it's like an airplane pilot requesting clearance for landing. Once granted, he alone can use the runway space. Only after he completes the landing and leaves the space can another pilot be granted use of the same space.

We are always thinking—filling that mental space—at least during our waking hours. If I ask you to stop thinking for a minute, you will have one of several reactions. Some of you will pick a spot on the wall and intently stare at it, others will try very diligently to make their minds a complete blank, perhaps even paint it black. Others will squeeze their eyes tightly shut, and others will hold their breath. (Passing out from lack of breath doesn't count.)

However, when we think, our thoughts can only be generated from one of three places. Imagine a large rectangle divided into thirds with the far left third representing the past, the far right representing the future, and the middle, the present. All thoughts will come from one of these three areas. Your body is always in the present—it is impossible for it to physically function in the past or the future. When your mind and body are in the same place, and concentrating on the same thing, you will get the best results because you are connected thinking-wise to what you are doing. During any type of performance, it is best to have your mind with your body in the moment. The highest degree of accomplishment occurs with the mind and the body in the present.

An athlete who finds himself in a mindset other than this will often make errors. Without concentrated effort, his body moves on through the rest of the routine, while his mind stays in the past wondering what went wrong. His body is left to operate without his mind to consciously guide him. His mind could even go into the future using that mistake as a predictor of outcome, reinforcing the error, and further weakening the power of his performance.

Again, take the example of the skater who is executing a double axle. Say that she does not make any conscious modification to the contents in her double axle filing cabinet. Her mind will go to the past and retrieve the information that is stored there. If, in fact, her very best jump was the double axle, she will be perfectly content with the stored information and not have any need or desire to change it. However, if she was not pleased with either the quality or consistency of her performance, she needs to know how to make the necessary mental changes to achieve a better jump.

The first step is to block the incoming message from the filing cabinet. To do that, she must consciously think of something else to keep the mental space occupied so past information from the filing cabinet cannot enter, while simultaneously correcting the problem. She must determine what she is doing and what she wants to do. For example, if her filing cabinet has a response pattern of not bringing her leg through when executing the jump, and she needs to bring her leg through, then, as she goes down the ice, she needs to repeat to herself the message command, "Leg through, leg through, leg through," until she has executed the jump. Continual repetition is crucial to this process. Otherwise, at a break in thought, the old information will move into the mental space and she will get the previous unsatisfactory result.

The reason for this is that the subconscious believes everything you tell it without question. It truly believes that it can best serve you by giving back the information you gave it. Your conscious mind can easily tell the difference between what is real and imagined, but your subconscious cannot. What is logged into your subconscious goes in as if it actually happened. Your subconscious mind will file negative and positive input equally believing that everything is accurate and valuable information whether it is or not.

So, at every opportunity during the reprogramming process, your subconscious will attempt to deliver the previously programmed mental command. If consistent repetition of the new command does not occur, information from your filing cabinet will enter and the contents of your mental space will look like this: "leg through, leg through, leg out, leg out, leg through," creating inconsistency. The result will almost surely be what you have previously done—leg out. If your mental space looks like this: "leg through, leg through, leg through," and continues that way through execution, your body will bring the leg through in fine form. In this particular example, there are only two reasons why the skater would not get the desired outcome of an improved jump: 1) the leg position was not really the problem, or, 2) she didn't say the new command over and over keeping the old command blocked. These same two reasons will keep you from having success with this technique when applied to other areas of your life. To achieve consistency in the conscious takes mental discipline; but developing that mental discipline will always increase your performance and achievements. These examples show the power of the mind as it directs the body. It demonstrates what happens if you continue operating on your original default settings rather than reprogramming those settings.

Another way to look at this concept is to have a friend walk with you through an example I use frequently when giving seminars and workshops. Ask your friend to put both of his arms out straight in front of him and, with his eyes closed, mentally follow along with you on a guided tour. Start telling him that the two of you are going to the grocery store to prepare for a get together this evening with your friends. As you enter the grocery store, you are going to slip a plastic bag, like the ones we frequently see in supermarkets, on his wrists. As you continue through the store, up and down the aisles, let him know that you are putting a jar of peanuts, a bag of cookies, a box of microwave popcorn, and some other party supplies in the bag on the right. As you turn one corner, you see flowers and helium balloons and decide to get a couple of balloons for decoration. After selecting two, suggest to him that you are going to tie them to his left wrist. You also notice some greeting cards and you remember to pick some up for a relative's birthday. You slip them into the bag on his left wrist. Stop and have your friend open his eyes. He will see what you observed while taking him through the guided imagery. His right arm will have moved towards the floor. His left arm will have risen toward the ceiling. He imagined the items in the right bag being heavy and the items on the left being light. Since the subconscious is controlled through the conscious, those thoughts were transmitted to his subconscious causing it to treat that information as fact and make his body respond accordingly.

Likewise, if I were to put a board on the floor and ask you to walk across it, your mind would create a picture telling you that you can easily and safely do that. If I were to move that board about three feet from the floor and again ask you to walk across it, you would create another picture. This time you sense that you need to go slowly and be careful because you could fall and get hurt. But, more likely, you could jump that distance without getting hurt if you did fall. If I were then to raise the board to over 10 feet in height, your created picture would be that you would definitely fall if you attempted to walk across it. In each of these examples, your mind created a picture of the situation, then attached feelings of being safe or being fearful.

Both of these examples show the interdependency between your thoughts, your feelings, and your behavior. Your thoughts determine how you are feeling and what your body is doing. If you want to find out why you are feeling the way you are, check out your thoughts or if you want to find our why you are behaving the way you are, check out your thoughts. You are what you think!

3

◆

Self-talk

Other than the information that was delivered to us in early childhood via our parents, experiences, role models, etc., there are two processes that transfer and carry information to the various filing cabinets we use to perform in all areas of our lives. These processes create additional content. These two processes are the way we fill and change the information in our files. Content is logged in through saying and seeing; the processes are self-talk and visualization. Visualization is seeing pictures in your head and self-talk is the dialogue that is going on in your head. If you learn only one mental performance skill from this book, the most important one would be the relationship between how we think and how we feel and behave. The difference between our best and worst performances lies within our mind and thoughts.

Self-talk is our continuous internal dialogue—we are literally talking to ourselves and telling ourselves what to think and feel about whatever is occurring. Since we have total control over what we think, what we choose to say to ourselves is one of our most important choices. Unfortunately, if there were a law against verbally abusing ourselves, we'd all be in jail. We continually repeat the negative thoughts that people and experiences have filed in our filing cabinets whether or not they are currently true.

It has been suggested that each of us has over 50,000 thoughts a day. That is significant input, especially when we remember that the quality and content of those 50,000 plus thoughts will impact how we see ourselves, how we feel about ourselves and our lives, and how we choose to behave.

The content of self-talk creates feeling, which then leads to behavior. It is impossible to have feelings without thoughts. So, if you ever wonder why you behave in a certain way, you can easily determine that by going back and checking out your feelings. After identifying those, go back and identify your thoughts. Then you will understand the reason for your behavior. Remember that it takes a series of thoughts to create feelings, then behavior. It cannot be done any other way.

Self-talk is instrumental in creating behavior only if a pattern has been created. Every-day self-talk is random and non-focused; however, it accumulates just as if it were purely intentional. We operate somewhat like the workings of the computer—a common saying is garbage in, garbage out. Whatever we continually log in from our self-talk is what we will get back. People become aware of their self-talk patterns when they experience something in their behavior that they do not like. This behavior encourages them to look at what they are saying to themselves. If you truly want to change what you are doing, you must first alter your thoughts.

Thoughts that determine undesirable behavior are either negative thoughts from early childhood or negative thoughts that we currently load in. Your current

21

negative self-talk comes from yourself directly or from your interpretation of what you hear other people say to you. For example, you may continually tell yourself that you did a poor job on a report. Or, after turning in the report, your manager tells you the report was fine quality except for spelling errors, but you choose to log that in as having done a poor job. Again, you will get back exactly what you load. Negative self-talk will become negative thinking and behavior; and positive self-talk will become positive thinking and behavior. Your subconscious does not have the ability to change your input from negative to positive. That has to be a conscious choice—to log in what you want to get out, or to block and reprogram what was previously input. As Henry Ford said, "Whether you think you can, or whether you think you can't, you are right."

Imagine that your mind is a fertile garden where the soil has been rotated and plowed and prepared for planting. Also, image that each time you have a negative thought, you are literally planting a weed into that space. Each time you have a positive thought, you are planting a flower. At the end of the day, check your plot of land

and see whether you have a group of weeds, a beautiful flower garden, or some mixture. You can be assured that if you have an abundance of flowers, you have been planting positive thoughts, you will be feeling happy and uplifted, and your behavior will indicate that. On the other hand, if you have an area overgrown with weeds, you can be assured that you have been sowing negative thoughts, will be feeling sad and depressed, and exhibiting negative behavior. A mixed garden (flowers and weeds) indicates that you are either in the process of changing your programming from positive to negative or negative to positive, an active choice on your part. Or it could simply mean that you are confused about how you really think about a particular issue.

Since the content of the filing cabinet determines performance response, which in turn affects and in some instances determines the result, we often let the result indicate whether or not to make changes. You cannot go into the past to rearrange the contents and make changes. Making changes in self-talk can only occur in the present. If you find an area for which you want to eliminate negative self-talk, one technique you might use is called "thought stopping." Thought stopping is recognizing that you are doing something you want to change and, as soon as you recognize it, you will literally say "stop" and replace the negative with a positive statement.

If you want to find out how frequently you are making negative self-talk statements to yourself about a certain issue, put a rubber band on your wrist for one day. On that day, pay particular attention to negative statements you are making. Each and every time that you make a negative statement or have a negative thought, pop the rubber band. The size of the welt at the end of the day will indicate the amount of your negative self-talk. This technique is very effective because controlling your negative self-talk is easier as you learn to recognize it when it's occurring.

It has been said that it takes eleven positive thoughts to cancel one negative thought about the same subject. So, when an athlete says to himself, "I'm not any good," he needs to say eleven different positive statements to himself about how good an athlete he really is to cancel that one negative statement. This process works the same way in any area of your life. It is highly unlikely that any of you will sit around and talk to yourself in that way; thus, the weed that was planted rapidly duplicates itself. Negative statements seem to come into being on their own, while positive ones require consistent attention to reproduce in good and positive ways. Thus, it seems to me that it would be a much better use of time and energy to develop skills to recognize and minimize negative self-talk rather than spending the time to overcome it once it has occurred.

Be assured that if you replace negative self-talk with positive self-talk, you will notice the difference in your sense of well being. You will eliminate the type of thinking that limits your behavior and capability. You will choose consciously to think in the present—the only place positive changes will be made. People who spend their time in the present are achievers and people who spend their time in the past or future are usually worriers.

Imagine that when you wake up every morning, you are given a box of energy. This energy must be used or thrown away at the end of the day. Approximately 7%

of the energy in that box should be allocated to thinking about the past. What your parents told you, that the past is over and done with and you can only learn from it, is true. Likewise, about 7% of that energy should be applied to the future. Other than general ideas (goals) about what you want to achieve in the future, you can do nothing more there, because the future will be determined by what you are doing or not doing in the present. The entire remaining energy is for use today only. This means that approximately 85% of the energy is available for today. Imagine what can be accomplished with that amount of focus!

Changing a pattern of negative self-talk requires a great deal of commitment. It is often shown that it takes 21 days to make or break a habit. You have to do something or not do something for 21 days in a row before your mind will accept it as reprogrammed. Anything short of that, your mind accepts as idle inconsistent chatter. Your subconscious says, "Just hold on, she'll get tired, this won't last very long." And, sure enough, this is often true. It's important to know that the 21 days must follow one another consecutively, stopping in between results in having to start again. Many people will make a three to five day effort toward change and will only keep the momentum going if they are getting profound results or are incredibly committed. Think about changes that you have tried to make. How often have you focused or concentrated on that change for twenty-one days in a row. If you did, you successfully made changes.

My personal experience with this concept helps me believe that this process of change is true. One year, having diligently made New Year's resolutions that I most often didn't keep, I committed (I thought) to adding exercise to my daily life. I acquired a membership to the local gym, purchased the proper attire—a little leotard and matching leggings—and off I went. I diligently pursued this course of action for twenty days, doing squats, leg lifts, whatever the instructor directed me to do. However, when I realized that I had been going for twenty days, I did not go on the twenty-first day. I was terrified that, if I went, it would become a habit, something that I'd have to do for the rest of my life. I happily, but consciously, let my behavior continue to be defined by the programming that was in my past.

An athlete uses the concept of positive self-talk in four ways to enhance performance. One way is the repetition of a technical command that was mentioned previously regarding the ice skater and her leg commands. The second way is to have her self-talk be motivational, such as, "Go, Go, Go," or, "I can do this!" The third way is to have self-talk be about feelings— "This is easy, this is fun." No matter which of these three an athlete uses, the commands should be a few simple words and if possible rhythmic.

The fourth form of self-talk is to have the dialogue create pictures or images of what you want to achieve. In this case, athletes might tell themselves to hold their arms in a position similar to hugging a tree or to pull their arms though in a scooping motion. This form of self-talk creates pictures, as does the picturing process called visualization. Visualization along with self-talk make up the two processes that transfer and carry information to the various filing cabinets that successful people use for performance in all areas of their lives.

4

◆

Visualization

Visualization is a process in which pictures and images are created in the mind's eye of what we want or hope to accomplish. It is a natural skill that people use all the time. We can learn to improve and build upon our present visualization abilities in order to enhance performance.

Visualization is an invaluable tool that we often use to achieve what we want. It has been used by many athletes like figure skater Brian Boitano with his 1988 Olympic win and golfer Jack Nicklaus during his six victories at the Master's. People use visualization to ask for a raise, prepare for a speaking engagement, or find a solution to a problem. In the medical field, Dr. Carl Simonton uses visualization intensely in his work with cancer patients. Successful people constantly and consistently use visualization. If you faithfully picture your dream or goal, it will reprogram you subconsciously, where changes occur, and work its way into your behavior.

Visualization prepares the body and mind for activity. This process creates movies. We then take the movies and play them out when we are ready to perform. Sometimes these movies are automatically created and sometimes we want to put special effort into creating them. This is especially true if we want to make changes in something we are doing or if we want to prepare ourselves for something we want to do. Visualization can help us prepare for situations in which we may normally be distracted and lose our focus or confidence.

When getting ready to perform in any of life's situations, you have a mental picture of what you think that will be like. This mental picture may not be something you literally see but, rather, one that you sense. This seeing or sensing allows your subconscious to begin preparing for the actual event. For instance, if you are preparing to give a talk, you might create a mental picture that says the room will be small, the audience will be small, and you will have a podium behind which you will stand as you give the talk. If you create that mental picture without facts, hoping the conditions will be as you envision them, you may be in for a rude awakening. As you enter the area, your conscious mind will take a picture of the room. You will cautiously notice that the room is very large, that there is a podium, but that the audience is very large. If this information is at odds with your mental picture, you can be thrown off track. Reality is not in line with your expectation. To avoid this kind of frustration, use visualization to prepare for several scenarios. Then you will be prepared for whatever awaits you on the day of the talk.

Use the fact that you have a picture in your mind of everything and anything you try to do to describe where you think you should be at any given time. Picture where you think you should be on a certain project or in your life, how much money you should be making, what kind of job you should have, how you should be treated, even how you should look and act. Remember that the closer behavior and reality match the established picture, the more content you are with your life. Conversely, the further you are from the picture, the more dissatisfied and unhappy you are. Therefore, create the most accurate and detailed picture of your expectations that you can. If these images are positive, they are likely to reduce pressure and enhance performance; if negative, they will increase pressure and interfere with performance. Positive visualization keeps the mind occupied and prevents distracting negative thoughts. It helps keep the focus on the task at hand.

Just as you are talking to yourself all the time, you are also creating pictures for yourself all the time. As these pictures are developed, they become prototypes for what your subconscious expects you to be doing consciously. When your conscious behavior does not line up with this prototype, you become uneasy or doubtful. On the other hand, creating detailed, accurate pictures or images of what you want or expect to do enhances your performance and creates confidence because you are doing what you saw yourself doing.

As I have mentioned, the subconscious takes in whatever is presented, via self-talk or visualization, as true and factual. It does not have the ability to discriminate. Pretend you are driving a car; someone rear-ends you and you get hurt. Like a camera with a wide-angle lens, your mind takes a picture of what you saw at the time of impact. That picture will be filed in your subconscious. Any time in the future that you see that picture, even a similar one, you will become fearful and anxious. Your subconscious is trying to protect you from more harm by warning you that the last time you saw this particular picture, you got hurt. In reality that is not true but your subconscious believes your pain was caused by the contents of the picture. Only through conscious awareness can you reprogram this response.

In fact, the mind will even indicate to the body that a particular physical skill is being done via the nervous system when in fact it is not. A classic example of this involves basketball players. Members of a team were divided into three groups. One group was told to practice free throws every day for twenty-one days while the second group was asked to visualize shooting free throws for the same amount of time. A third group did neither. Each group was assessed on the first and last day to determine improvement. The results indicated that the players who were shooting the basketball practicing free throws had improved approximately 24% while those who visualized but never actually shot free throws had improved 23%. Why? Because as we visualize a physical activity, our mind sends electrical impulses to the same muscles that would be used if we were actually doing the activity.

A researcher in England found that by using mental skills alone muscle strength could be improved by 16%. This means that sitting in a chair and doing a workout in our head will have an effect on our muscles. In this study, the focus was on an isolated muscle in the little finger but, since all muscles work the same way, the findings apply to other parts of the body as well.

Just as our behavior is a result of our accumulated patterns of self-talk, our behavior is dictated by the pictures or images that we have created. An athlete who sees himself hitting the golf ball in a certain way or running very fast will be able to perform much better than one who cannot see himself performing well. In fact, in all areas of life, we usually do what we can see ourselves doing. Oftentimes, you will even hear people say, "Oh, I can't see myself doing that," when asked to participate in an activity. So, people who enjoy snorkeling can imagine themselves snorkeling. People who are public speakers can see themselves speaking. If you can picture or imagine yourself doing it, then you can do it.

It is this picturing or imaging idea that sometimes confuses people. Some people expect the imagined pictures to look like the pictures on a movie screen. That could be true. But you may also see stick figures, or not actually see but rather sense something. How you see is not as important as adding details and attaching emotions to the image. Many elite and world class athletes can tell you, with heart-felt emotion, each and every detail of the picture they have been following on their way to becoming successful. Among people generally, many will say that they knew when they were very young that they were going to be a fireman, a teacher, a nurse, because of the images of themselves they saw through the years.

Perhaps one of the most dramatic examples of the power of visualization relates to a golfer who usually shot in the nineties. Circumstances kept him from playing for seven years. The next time on the course after that long seven-year break, he shot 74. During those seven years, he did not take any golf lessons and his physical ability deteriorated—he was housed in a small cage as a prisoner of war. For five-and-a-half years he was in isolation. After several months of praying for his release, he decided to figure out a way to survive. He chose to mentally play golf while in his cage. He played eighteen holes every day for all seven of those years and visualized every tiny detail that he could imagine—course, weather, clothes, trees, tees, and pin placement. He then imagined every detail of holding each club, keeping his eye on the ball, his back swing and follow through, the flight of the ball and where it landed. The eighteen holes he played mentally and visually took the same time as when he actually played—about four hours.

After not playing golf for seven years, and under these horrible conditions, he cut fifteen strokes off his game. This is the power of visualization as it is practiced without pressure, leading to a better performance when there is pressure.

To look at your visualization skills, imagine an orchard with row after row after row of trees heavily laden with red apples. On the ground are many other apples in various states. Some broke into pieces when they fell from the tree, some look rotten, and some look like they recently fell from the tree and are in good shape. Notice the slight breeze that lightens the heat of the day. Imagine yourself walking up to one of the trees, looking at the ground, and seeing the apples. Now, look up above your head and notice that there is a bright red apple immediately to your right. Reaching out your right hand, pick the apple. Look closely at the apple and notice the stem with two green leaves attached to it. Slowly turn the apple, notice a wormhole, and see if you can travel inside the apple and look out through the wormhole.

After experiencing this guided imagery, evaluate

whether or not you could easily picture the images, details, and feelings. To visualize effectively, you must be able to concentrate and fix your mind on one thought or image. If you did that quite well, you are already aware of, and probably using, one of the most powerful mental skills relating to successful performances.

People who make visualization a habit know that it is valuable to do this daily for a minimum of 21 days before an actual performance. They know that they need to visualize their performances correctly and change anything that is not accurate. They know that some components may need to be repeated. In trying to visualize as vividly as possible, sights, sounds, and touch need to be included. It is best to learn visualization when you are calm and relaxed, when you can use all of your senses, when you can control your images, and when you can add movement to imagery. The best time to access the subconscious part of the mind is during those first hours after awakening in the morning when your mind is more open to new programming than any other time of day. The next best time is while you are drifting off to sleep. Ten to fifteen minutes a day should be spent working on imagery, preferably at a particular time that is set aside for this purpose.

Another interesting and helpful approach to visualization is spending about 80% of your visualization time focusing on your response to anticipated conditions and 20% on how you would respond to surprises or unanticipated conditions. Follow each situation to a successful conclusion.

Visualization skills are very helpful for achieving your goals. They can be used to motivate you to train, to psyche yourself up, to learn better movement, to refocus, and to prepare. You will be assured of enhancing your performance in all areas of your life by consistently and appropriately using visualization skills.

5

◆

The files and how they work

We are always doing; we are always performing. Performance is not just on a stage or a playing field. It occurs everyday, on a regular basis, as a normal part of life. When we discuss an issue with our spouse, communicate with our neighbor, interact with our children, interview for a job, give a lecture or sales presentation for our company, or compete in a sanctioned sports competition, we are performing.

In sports, business, and other areas of our lives, we have goals that we want to accomplish when we perform.

We seek the outcome of these goals. Whether we are moving toward the outcome or beyond the outcome, we employ performance responses. When our performance responses take us beyond an outcome, we establish performance responses toward the next outcome. Once an outcome is known, change occurs and the never-ending, ongoing process continues.

In order to deal effectively with change, you must know and recognize your personal response patterns as well as how to make necessary adjustments in them. Personal response patterns have their origins in childhood and will remain as they were formed unless changed through conscious choice via self-talk and visualization which was explained in chapters three and four. This change almost always comes about as a result of not being satisfied with what is presently happening in your sports, business, or personal life.

Each of you has individual skills that control the caliber of your performances. As explained in chapter two, these skills are housed in filing cabinets in the subconscious part of your mind. They are constantly at work using their contents to help you perform in every situation or interaction you encounter. In some cases these responses will be effective and sometimes not. Some will be highly effective and produce almost precisely the outcomes that you desire. You will be able to quickly differentiate the ones that need to be left alone from those that need to be updated to produce more effective outcomes.

The remarkable thing about these files is that, regardless of their condition, they function and guide your performances at all times. You may be pleased with the type of performances that you have due to the files' input, or you may be displeased. Regardless, it is critically important to be aware of the content of each and be able to have the skills and knowledge necessary to make changes to the files when needed.

In the following chapters, these performance files are identified and explained. The information will enable you to improve those that are less productive than you want them to be. Remember: you use the contents of these files to determine your response. Thus, content is the stored information itself, while response is the displayed behavior formed by the content. You are in charge of the content; thus, you are in charge of your response.

Responses allow others to make assumptions about your goal setting and other performance skills. They are observable characteristics. What you present outwardly is in these response settings, whether you know it or not. Your choice is to either continue in your default settings with rapid responses, or, to slow down, take your time, change your thinking, and change your responses. Think of the original settings as the default. They are not necessarily bad. But it is critical to know what they are. Don't just live life on your default settings. Runners need coaches, training, and practice to expand their original settings and talent. This is an ongoing process. Adjusting to changes is a huge part of preparation and training. Variables continue to change. We each learn to respond to different variables depending on our early life experience. For example, if you never saw anyone set goals, deal with fear, or make mistakes, your default settings don't give you a clue as to how to do this. So you must create new, appropriate settings.

When creating new settings, you will use information from each of the files. These files don't work singularly, but rather in combination. However, they will be presented in separate chapters in order to understand them more clearly. Furthermore, the file chapters are arranged so their inter-relatedness and flow is readily apparent. I did this in much the same manner as the Mother Goose nursery rhyme, "For want of a nail, the shoe was lost. For want of a shoe, the horse was lost," where one thing affects another and on and on and on. All is connected. Likewise, all of these files are connected; you will use information from each of them every time you perform or seek to improve an area of your life.

It is necessary to formulate goals, which if achieved would accomplish your desired improvements. The goals are accomplished through concentration. However, perfectionism can easily sabotage even the best of goals if you cannot handle making mistakes or the effects of change. Change, whether positive or negative, will create stress but it can be dealt with

45

effectively through communication by identifying and sharing your feelings or moods.

At this point, you will experience some level or form of fear. You will need to relax, continue working toward your goals, and manage your time effectively to create a more satisfied and balanced life.

By becoming skilled at the processes in this book, you will accomplish your goals and your newly formulated self-image could lead you to another area that you want to improve. Thus, the high performance thinking begins again. This is a pattern similar to the ongoing painting of the Golden Gate Bridge where a team begins painting and when they get to the end of the job they simply begin again

Remember that based on the information in your files, you are capable of doing anything you want to do and that self-talk can override any negative information you have in your filing cabinets. These are your tools for success. What you have in these files, and therefore how you respond, will determine how great your success will be.

6

◆

File: Self-image

Massive research indicates that your single most
important characteristic is how you feel about yourself.
Self-image is considered to be 85% attitude and 15%
facts or skills. People who genuinely like and accept
themselves are valuable individuals who perform at a
higher level of effectiveness than others. William James
has said that the greatest discovery of his generation
was that a human being could alter his life by altering
his attitude.

Our self-image or self-concept is how we think
and feel about ourselves. This is based on our thoughts
and other's thoughts that have been previously logged

into our filing cabinets. These thoughts have created and formed certain feelings about ourselves that lead us to behave in certain ways. Our programming has been a combination of positive and negative experiences. If we have accumulated a lot of positive input in our files, we have felt loved and valued and were positively influenced by those around us, like family, friends, teachers, and other role models who encouraged us in our efforts. These positive experiences gave us a sense of confidence.

As a result, we will likely present ourselves confidently as a person who is positive, who understands herself, and who knows what she wants. The opposite input (negative) results in presenting ourselves as one who lacks confidence, is pessimistic, acts awkward, and feels insignificant.

What people learn about us and what we learn about other people is approximately 87% from sight, so how we present ourselves is very important. We need to let people see that we feel confident about ourselves and our actions whether we are hitting a tennis ball, landing a jump on the ice, or giving a presentation at our company. We also need to present ourselves confidently because about 55% of the way people respond to us is through their reading of our body language.

A lot of the information in our self-image filing cabinet which creates our behavior was literally poured into us by our family, teachers, friends, and life experiences. In too many cases we are responding from that input and haven't looked at the information to see if we agree with it or if it's still true today. Too often, we find ourselves living with this limiting information. We need to learn how to think in new and different ways. It's like knowing that the information you seek is inside a dark room and you want to see it. You walk into the room and flick on the light switch. Nothing happens. After checking, you find that the only thing wrong is that the light bulb has burned out; otherwise, the room would be full of light. Rather than stand there and repeatedly flip the switch waiting for the room to be lit, you would change the light bulb. Likewise, you need to change your light bulbs if you are not getting the results you want from the way you respond to things. You need to change the way you see or think about things.

We all have old limiting beliefs about who we are. They once fit in our lives, but we have outlived their usefulness and they have become limiting in the present. They no longer serve us. Holding on to behaviors and emotions that hold you back creates stress, increases fear, and interferes with your self-image. Some of these are anger, approval seeking, hiding feelings, perfectionism, rejecting compliments, blaming others, and always having to be in control. When you release these outdated behaviors and emotions, and draw in those that will serve you better today, you will more successfully achieve your goals; thus changing your self image.

Self-image or self-concept is made up of four parts. The first part is how we see ourselves; part two is how others see us; part three is how we think others see us; and part four is how we'd like to be. The greatest gift we can give or receive is part two—how others see us—since they almost always see us better than we see ourselves. Others view and perceive us in the now, the present, without filters, while we view ourselves through the filters of all our past images and knowledge.

Keeping the four parts of our self-image intact and feeling very together is much like trying to have toddler quadruplets line up in single file and stay that way for a period of time. Like the toddlers, something or some part is always moving and throwing us off balance as we learn and grow, or as we become fearful, doubtful, or think negatively. Up and down cycles are normal as long as they do not occur continuously or with great force as they can create an unsettling shift in our self-concept that alters our idea of ourselves causing us to perform poorly.

In the fourth part of our self-image, it is especially important that our goals line up with our picture of who we would like to be or what we'd like to be doing. Otherwise we will find ourselves expressing actions and behaviors that are consistent with our self-image but are not consistent with those required for achieving our goals. Remember, it is very difficult if not impossible to be successful at something that we can't see ourselves doing or something that we really don't want to do or be.

How we measure or evaluate ourselves is very important; therefore, it is necessary to use appropriate yardsticks to do the measuring. Without using appropriate ones, you can skew your self-image which in turn can skew your behavior. For instance, if an athlete measures his performance against a higher level athlete who performs more advanced technical skills, he will always come up short and sense failure. On the other hand, if he measures himself against someone who is clearly below his skill level, he will always look better then he really is and both instances can create false expectations of his performances. Since we will always perform in a way that is consistent with how we see ourselves, it is important that our self-image be as accurate as possible.

We all have the same opportunity to think and reprogram our self-image to behave in ways that create more success. This process is available to all of us. Some choose to accept this opportunity and work with it. Others choose to block the process. Those who choose to block the process would probably benefit from handing out pre-printed cards to everyone that says, "Hello, my name is John and this is how I am." He is saying, in effect, "I have no interest in developing the mental skills that will teach me how to do something about becoming more like who I aspire to be."

Confidence is a result of a healthy self-image. It creates a belief that says we have the ability to do a certain skill necessary to create a performance outcome. Confidence is a feeling that we are able to do what we need to do when we need to do it. It is learned, cumulative, and dependent on our past experiences. Relationships exist between confidence, and performance. There is a range that goes from no confidence, to having confidence, to being over confident. This means that as confidence increases so does performance, except at that point where confidence increases too much in relation to performance; then performance decreases as concentration decreases.

People with a high level of confidence may have as many weaknesses as people with lower self-esteem. The difference is that, instead of dwelling on their handicaps, confident people compensate by building on their strengths and focusing on their positive accomplishments. How you view and file your performances are significant to the development of your self-confidence. One technique that works well in changing your viewpoint from failure to success is the following. Skaters are required to do about ten elements in their short program and they repeatedly practice the entire program. Our skater tends to miss one or two elements, sometimes none at all. However, each time she leaves the ice she says to herself that she did not have a clean program and feels unsuccessful. She will begin feeling more and more like a failure, her performance will be affected, and her self-image will be diminished.

She clearly needs to log in these practices differently. For example, she can assign a value of ten points to each element since the total of ten would then add up to 100. After completing each run through, she would add the points for the elements she successfully completed and would see that each time she scored 100 or 90 or 80. Since she already has the notion that 100 is excellent, 90 is very good, and 80 is still doing well, she will begin to see that her practice performances are, in fact, very successful. Her confidence and self-image will be enhanced and her performances will become more consistent.

Someone once said, "You cannot be given a life by someone else. Of all the people you will know in a lifetime, you are the only one you will never leave or lose. To the question of your life, you are the only answer. To the problems of your life, you are the only solution." I would only add that today, in relationship to high performance thinking, you too are the answer and the solution.

7

◆

File: Goals

Goal setting is the ability to create a plan of action that allows you to choose where you want to go and what you want to achieve in life. It gives you long-term vision and short-term motivation.

Your perception about goal setting was gleaned from childhood experiences in school, home, and play. If you experienced family goal setting that was vague, disorganized, or sporadic, then you won't understand the importance of goals or the achievement resulting from goals. Nor will you be able to create goals for yourself. The major benefits of goal setting have not occurred for you.

Most people do have a minimum ability to set goals because they learned in childhood that things do not happen just by saying so. Each activity/goal had a plan of action with it, whether a birthday celebration, a family trip, or the purchase of a car.

If you had many disappointing childhood experiences and you could determine that something did not occur because of a lack of preplanning, such as a missed time frame, insufficient information, or lack of knowledge, then, most likely, you will be a great believer in goal setting. You will want to avoid feeling that same disappointment in your adult life.

From childhood experience, you know that identifying a large goal is relatively easy; identifying smaller goals that help accomplish larger ones is more difficult. Effective goal setting should have more emphasis on immediate goals. These short-term goals may even need to be broken down into daily, weekly, or monthly ones. These smaller immediate goals need to be specific and performance (action) based rather than outcome (results) based.

All goals need to be realistic; otherwise, you will set long range or immediate ones that are unrealistically high, based upon inaccurate or insufficient information, other people, or an expectation that you are going to perform your best every time. They can be too low because you fear failure or because you are not willing to take risks and stretch yourself. Ideally, goals are set so that performance is slightly out of your immediate grasp, but not so far that there is no hope of achieving them. People will not put a lot of hard work and effort into a goal that they don't feel is realistic.

Often, people need to rid themselves of self-defeating thoughts about goal setting. Rethink goal setting by accepting the following principles. Small performance goals will change behavior. Goal setting tells you where you need to go, how to get there, and when you are making progress. It encourages you to keep going. The more skilled you are at creating a goal, the better the goal will be and the better the chance you will have of achieving it. Goal setting has been found to improve performance because it increases motivation, improves training, and improves self-confidence. It assures that you will have direction and feedback.

Vague goals are practically useless. Some people set goals by making statements like, "I want to run faster, swim faster, give better talks." But the person who has studied goal setting knows that the components that create the best goals are measurable units, i.e., "to be able to run faster I will sprint three times a week for twenty minutes." Specifics guarantee feedback. You can then adjust the goal if needed.

Specifics will assure that your goals will be performance based rather than outcome based. Goals based on outcomes are susceptible to tampering by things beyond your control. You should have as much control over your goals as possible. If an athlete was going to a national competition, a performance goal would be, "I will attempt every triple jump in my program." An outcome goal would be, "I will finish first or second." We know that a person can try every triple jump and do well. But we still cannot predict the outcome of the competition for a variety of reasons

beyond our control—judging, other athletes' performances, choreography, ice conditions.

If you are giving a presentation to a company, and
your goal is to give the best talk on marketing that
day—which is an outcome goal—you have created a
goal over which you have very little control. If you
based your goal on presenting a complete, five-step
marketing strategy plan—a performance goal—and
you do so, you retain control over achievement of your
goal. Remember, set goals that give you as much control as possible.

Any goal should improve or change your behavior
because its intent is to make you better, whether to lose
weight, quit smoking, learn another technical skill, or
get a promotion. Effective goals need to be positive,
precise, and written. Definite written goals and a plan
for achieving them not only indicates a willingness to
grow and perform better, but practically assures you of
being more successful. Otherwise, you will be in a position similar to Alice when she approached the fork in
the road and sought directions from the Cheshire cat.

Upon approaching the cat, she asked him whether she should go to the left or to the right. Before he could answer, he wanted to know where it was she wanted to go. Alice replied that she had no idea where she wanted to go. The cat informed her that it really didn't matter then whether she went to the right or to the left.

8

◆

File: Concentration

Concentration is the ability to stay focused on certain moves and activities that will create a completed performance. Tangent to concentration is the ability to refocus when you have taken time out to address one of the many distractions that are everywhere. There is nothing wrong with distractions, the issue is how long you stay distracted. You need to recognize that you are distracted and get right back on track. For example, if a person is performing a task and their mind wanders to check out something else that is going on, and they have the ability to then refocus on the task, that person has successful concentrating and refocusing skills. However, too many people move away from the task at hand to check out what is going on and let their minds stay distracted; they linger, and stay so long that they have missed the opportunity to get back on task. In many incidents with athletes, or in our business or personal lives, this can make a huge difference in determining whether we are successful or not. A multitude of things compete for our attention every second and we will automatically concentrate where our interest is the highest. One way to work with your attentiveness is to see what you are concentrating on while also taking the time to find out what things are pulling you out of the moment and why.

How you concentrate and refocus is a learned skill. In early life, you learned to complete a task or not complete it. You either learned how to tune things out and focus on a single dimension, or you paid attention to everything around you and experienced difficulty concentrating. You may have had childhood experiences where the acceptable behavior was to not follow through—picking up your toys, completing projects, reading a book, completing sentences. Or, you may have been taught that it was necessary to follow through and complete each task. Regardless, you became comfortable with one process or the other.

Another aspect of concentration is whether or not you feel the need to be keenly aware of all the elements in your personal space in order to feel emotionally, mentally, and/or physically safe. If, during childhood, you experienced a situation where something seemed like it blind-sided you, and it was painful or traumatic, you would probably feel that if you had only had been aware of more factors, you could have prevented it and kept yourself safe. As a result, you developed antennas that scan your environment 24 hours a day, seven days a week, concentrating on as many factors as possible. You will spend so much time on this process that it will be very difficult to achieve your goals.

You could also have been raised in an environment where your every need was anticipated and taken care of by others and today you are surprised that you need to concentrate on and attend to certain elements in your personal space to feel emotionally, mentally and/or physically safe. You will also experience great difficulty in accomplishing your goals as you will be thrown off course by the many things that you did not anticipate.

Distractions are around us all the time, everywhere. There are two distractions that we are born with: the fear of falling and the fear of noise. They will interfere with our concentration. They are innate. They won't go away. The only thing we can do is learn to be aware of them. For instance, regardless of what you are doing—a golfer putting, a business man conducting an interview, talking on the phone with a friend, or a figure skater performing a jump—upon hearing a loud noise your mind will immediately check out the source of the noise and instantly decide whether you are physically safe. If you determine that you are safe, your mind can immediately return to what you were doing; but if you determine that you are not, you will focus on becoming safe.

Obviously, depending upon the type of performance, these built in distractors of falling and noise may or may not be a problem. For example, natural instinct tells us to put our hands out when we fall. In tennis this may not be a problem, but in figure skating, it would be a deduction from your score. In your personal life, a loud noise may not interfere with your talking on the phone with a friend, but, in giving a presentation or seminar, both you and your audience would be distracted and would need to refocus on the information being presented.

Like the three little bears with their porridge—too hot, too cold, or just right—we either pay too much, not enough, or an appropriate amount of attention to details. If you want to find out whether your concentration skills are helpful to you or not, first determine whether you pay appropriate or inappropriate (too little, too much) attention to details. In either case, you are focusing more on distractions than on the task at hand. So, if you find in a project or an athletic move that several steps were left out, you are paying too little attention to details. On the other hand, if you're trying to figure out precisely where your right leg needs to be during a golf swing, you may be paying too much attention to detail. Both keep you from giving your best performance.

A second way to determine whether the contents of your concentration file are effective is to think about whether you have a tendency to leave tasks open-ended and not completed. This indicates a problem with concentration and you need to practice distraction control. If you focus on what might be wrong, if you are in the past or the future, if you move to another task before completion of the current one, you mentally jump around and don't have appropriate skills for dealing with distractions. You have not taken time to identify possible distractions or taken time to plan ways to eliminate them.

A good method for correcting this problem is twofold: one, imagine and make a list of the situations or people who could distract you and figure out a plan for dealing with each. Two, practice some techniques for improving your level and time of concentration. One such technique would be to stare at a certain place on the wall and see how long you can keep your focus. Another would be to say the alphabet backwards. Yet another would be to practice moving rapidly back and forth from narrow to wide range focusing.

For instance, skaters may rapidly move from a narrow focus—the immediate ice and its condition, or their boot and shoestrings—to a wider range—the whole sheet of ice—to determine whether they will be in the correct place to perform a certain jump. This works much like a camera lens that moves from a normal range to create a close-up shot, then back to normal.

Another way to deal with distractions is to literally program yourself to believe, "Any distractions that I encounter other than those related to my physical safety, I will think about and determine what to do with after my performance." Distractions occur when something enters our space that we are not expecting or have not accounted for during our preparation. The more potential distractions a person can identify and deal with prior to performance, the smoother and more effective that performance will be.

Remember that distractions are everywhere and that there is nothing wrong with them. Remind yourself that distractions don't have to bother you. Expect that different things are going to happen and expect that you will be okay with them. The more you have identified a plan for handling distractions, the less likely you will be thrown by them. You can train yourself to rapidly check out the distraction and get right back on track.

For instance, you are asked to give a slide presentation at an upcoming conference and request the appropriate equipment. You can easily be thrown out of your comfort zone if you discover that there is no audio visual equipment in the room and you don't know who is responsible for obtaining it. Another example occurs when an athlete usually performs in an arena which has rows of seats numbered vertically from 1 through 50. When she goes to perform in another arena and sees seats in rows of 1 through 250, she feels overwhelmed and is distracted from her performance.

Both of these examples create fear, doubt, and anxiety. In each case, the distraction could have been recognized and dealt with prior to the performance. The speaker could have checked out the room previously or requested the name of the person responsible should any problems occur, while the athlete could check out the size and layout of every arena before performing. By doing the pre-check they assure themselves that they will not encounter an aspect of their performance picture that will distract them.

Not only is it important to understand concentration and the relevance of distractions, it is also important to know how to refocus after you have been distracted. A simple way is to return to basics. Whether you are an athlete or a speaker, you have a primary focus to return to. Think about what it is, overall, that you are trying to do—hit the ball, land a jump, give a talk, or interview for a job. You may also want to visualize yourself getting back on track again; but, remember that in order to visualize effectively, you must be able to concentrate, to fix your mind on one thought or image and keep it there.

You can also focus on an immediate goal which is a component of your primary focus. The immediate goal is part of the whole. The athlete might concentrate on the rotation part of a jump. The businessman might concentrate on the third section of a proposal he is writing. In both cases, reassure yourself that you are trained and ready by reminding yourself how many times you have done this particular skill. Take a minute to recall your past best performances and the feelings associated with them. By doing this, you are focusing on your immediate task rather than worrying about distractions that may come. You will stay in the moment, in the now. This intensifies your focus so that you are really connected to your moves or what you are doing in the present.

Simple reminders can be used to bring your mind back on target. These simple reminders should dominate your thoughts so you can create the narrow focus of attention mentioned earlier. Concentration is more powerful when you narrow the focus of your thoughts rather than when you have a wide range approach of four or five thoughts. Think of this as triangular learning. The broad base of the triangle represents all the details you have been shown while learning skills and techniques. The mind then begins combining all of these movements into chunkier movements. As you move up the triangle, you continue the combining process until finally all the combined movements result in a polished technical skill. You are now at the top of the triangle, the skill is a habit and you just do it. When you get to the top, you only need to think of one or two specific things to accomplish the skill rather than all of the pieces needed earlier. For instance, as a golfer begins to develop her swing, she would focus on many parts of the body and where they are at any particular moment—head, arms, legs, and upper body. As she begins to assimilate all of the movement, she develops a motion with all parts of her body moving as one until, finally, as she reaches the apex of the triangle, she now simply does a golf swing without focusing on all of the little pieces. Everything has become automatic.

9

◆

File: Perfectionism

We need to accept that making mistakes is a natural and normal part of any learning process and that bouncing back from mistakes and setbacks is a learned skill. We need to act as if making mistakes are the norm rather than the exception. Mistakes expand and teach us. Skills come from the experience gained from making mistakes.

Learning from your mistakes is critical to growth and development. Very successful people have a higher than ordinary tolerance for making mistakes. They know that setbacks occur; they expect them and deal with them. People who try to be perfect in sports or life constantly fail because it is impossible to be perfect.

Everyone needs a mistake quota that says, "While I am learning this particular skill, it is perfectly acceptable for me to make mistakes." That way you will be more relaxed and comfortable while you attempt a new jump or new way to hold your golf club because you understand that making a mistake is part of the learning process. A good rule of thumb is to expect to make one to three mistakes out of every ten attempts while in the learning mode.

Carl Jung, a psychoanalyst, says, "Perfection belongs to the gods; the most that we can hope for is excellence." Perfectionism is actually irrational thinking. There is no way we can always do what we attempt perfectly. People who have perfectionist viewpoints are often procrastinators because it is difficult to start something if they carry the belief that they will not be successful. Change your thoughts about being perfect. Reframe how you think by saying that success has its ups and downs. You can't be on every time and every day. Mistakes are a part of learning and should be expected. Mistakes are our teachers.

As with the other mental skills used for performance, the way a person, athlete, or businessman handles stress, success, failure, and making mistakes is a result of what they learned from parents and others around them. A lot of people learned that, if they just work or try hard enough, they can avoid dealing with failure. Having worked with top-ranking Olympic athletes as well as top-ranking business professionals, I can assure you that everyone makes mistakes and deals with failure in some way. Both provide opportunities for improvement.

Mistakes do not exist in the present. It is only after doing something that did not turn out the way we wanted that we determine we have made a mistake. It becomes a mistake after the doing. It's what we say to ourselves after we realize that we could have or should have done something differently. Mistakes are related to our expected outcomes.

For example, you pick out a color to paint a room while in a present state of mind. After you apply the paint to the wall, it is not what you expected or wanted.

Your choice of paint color then becomes a mistake. Or, a tennis player decides to place the ball barely over the net. The receiving player returns the ball and gains a point. Afterwards the strategy is viewed as a mistake. In both instances, there was nothing wrong with the choice, and it should not be interpreted as having made a mistake. Just because we didn't get what we expected, doesn't mean that how we went about it was wrong.

Mistakes of any sort need to be looked at, learned from, then dealt with in much the same way we choose to make a sandwich. This means that you would imagine that the bottom slice of bread is all the successes you have had during many practices and performances. Making mistakes is the filling, or the middle part. If you do not respond positively to this middle part, you are focusing extra attention on this and are always reminded of glaring mistakes. You have created an open-faced sandwich. If you add the other slice of bread, you sandwich in the failure or mistakes, thereby recognizing that failure and making mistakes is a normal part of life.

10

◆

File: Change

Individuals who most successfully meet their goals seek or welcome change. They do not resist it, they learn to flow with it. Those who cannot tolerate change well will often experience large amounts of stress and anxiety. Explore the content of your mind and see whether it is fearful and doubtful or open and free—whether you resist change or flow with change.

When you are dealing with issues in any area of your life, you have two choices. You can accept what is happening and where you are or you can change it. You can't do both. You may be doing some things that indicate you are accepting what is occurring while equally doing some behavior that would indicate you are trying to make changes. You will remain stuck while attempting to do both. You need to focus on doing one or the other—accept or change.

To either accept or change issues in your life usually requires getting rid of old thoughts, beliefs, and ideas that hold you back. People often have difficulty accepting things because they believe that to accept something is to like it. In reality, acceptance means simply acknowledging its existence or presence. People have difficulty making changes due to fear. It's been said that Michelangelo created sculpture by seeing his task as getting rid of the excess marble surrounding his creation. You, too, need to get rid of excess thinking that stands in the way of making the changes necessary for achieving higher performances.

We fear change even though we so desperately want it. Viktor Frankl in his book, *Man's Search for Meaning,* writes about his fellow prisoners in a Nazi concentration camp. Some of the prisoners, though wanting desperately to be free, had been held captive for so long that, when released, they walked out into the sunlight, blinked nervously, then silently walked back into the darkness of the prison. This is a situation that, in much less dramatic ways, we all experience at some time in our lives.

We all have secure places or comfort zones that were created from having consistency in our lives. We like what is familiar and what feels safe, and often spend a lot of time and energy maintaining that safe space. Goldfish react similarly. If we decide to clean the small tank that the goldfish live in, and while doing so, put the goldfish in a bathtub filled with water, they will swim around within the same circumference as that of their small tank. Instead of frolicking and playing in the entire bathtub, they stay within their comfort zone. We need to be willing to expand a little and be willing to take risks. Most of the time taking risks can create delightful new experiences and feelings. Successful people are risk-takers.

When you work on change and feel uncomfortable, strange, and awkward, you know you are moving toward accomplishing your goal because you are out of your comfort zone. When you no longer feel that healthy anxiety and have yet to achieve your goals, you are in trouble because you have quit working on change and are back to where you were—in your comfort zone.

When you become too comfortable, you create a stifling and rigid attitude toward change. You experience great stress when change does occur. There is no doubt that change will happen no matter how carefully you try to avoid it, so it's important to become more comfortable with the process. It has been said that change is inevitable—the only constant is change.

Like the other areas in your filing cabinets, you are following what was programmed as you were growing up. For the most part, you are following these scripts and you need to be able to assess whether they are good or bad, positive or negative. It's not what you do occasionally that changes your life; it's what you do consistently. Initially, you make your habits; then your habits make you. As you become aware, you can make desired changes. Awareness begins the process.

Life is change and change is part of life. If you have a positive attitude toward change, you will always respond more comfortably to changes that occur. The more positive your attitude toward change, the more stress resistant you will be. You must also remember that as you progress through change, your experiences may be similar to the growth of a Chinese bamboo tree. The Chinese bamboo tree needs to be watered and fertilized daily. Although you do this each and every day, it doesn't grow. But, if you do this daily for five years, all of a sudden, in six weeks time, it grows 90 feet. Although your growth is not going to be that dramatic, it is remarkable all the same. Day after day after day, you need to visualize, rework your thoughts, and try out new skills as you go through change. You will often think that you are never going to accomplish your goal or learn how to do a new skill. Then, one day, it comes together, and you can feel the growth. This process takes a great deal of patience and belief. And, of course, it is not that it just came together one day, it was because of all the hours spent on skill development. Just like all the days that someone watered that tree so it would eventually grow.

11

◆

File: Stress

One of the most common problems that all of us at all ages encounter is stress. Stress is an everyday fact of life that we cannot avoid. Almost everyone thinks they know what stress is. But relatively few really understand it, recognize what it does within their bodies, or know how to control it and live with it.

Stress is a term borrowed from physics and engineering where it is identified as a force of significant magnitude to distort or deform when applied to a system. Stress in its medical usage was coined by Hans Selye, a professor at the University of Montreal, and refers to any change that we must adjust to. While we tend to think of stressful events as being negative, stress can also be positive. However, we rarely hear of people becoming ill because their life and all of its parts are going wonderfully well. But, anything positive or negative can become stressful if it is strong enough, lasts too long, or is repeated too often. These causes or sources that lead to stress are called stressors.

We experience stressors from three basic areas: our environment, our body, and our thoughts. Our environment constantly has us adjusting to weather, noise, crowded conditions, time pressures, etc. Aging, poor diet, and sleep disturbances force our bodies to undergo physiological changes. How we interpret and label our experiences from these sources either relaxes or stresses us.

All of these sources create stress-producing situations or changes that our bodies must adapt to which automatically trigger a fight or flee response. This is an innate reaction we have to situations and events. Our regulating centers give the body information to prepare us for confronting and dealing with the situation or leaving the situation. Our pupils enlarge, our hearing becomes more sensitive, the blood rushes from our extremities to the trunk of our bodies, and we become tense and anxious.

Imagine a scene that we have probably all experienced at one time or another. You are driving on the interstate going a little over the speed limit. You are relaxed and comfortable until you look in the rearview mirror and notice that a patrol car with its light flashing is moving rapidly in your direction. You immediately go into your "fight or flee" response pattern experiencing the bodily changes. You remain in this state if the patrol car pulls you over and issues a ticket. However, if the patrol passes by, you immediately sense that the event is over and your body begins returning to its natural relaxed state.

You can't escape all the stresses of life or completely turn off your innate fight or flee response, but you can learn to counteract your habitual reaction to stress by learning to relax and by learning to return your body to its natural balanced state.

You cannot control external sources of stress but

you can identify and control stressors that come from within. When you attempt to reduce stress by not actively identifying the source of the stress, you are simply putting a Band-Aid on the problem. It is important to make a list of your major stressors, then determine whether they are issues that you can or cannot do something about. Your energy and focus should be on those over which you have some control.

Some of the most effective and positive ways to deal with stress are: exercise, proper eating habits, effective time management, and controlling your thinking by changing negative thoughts to positive ones. It also lowers stress if you don't turn molehills into mountains by being a worrywart, if you set realistic goals, and if you make sure at least one part of your life is in order.

Another way to help with stress is to imagine that every day you have a paper cup in your mind that holds all the stress of a particular day. Each night, look at the cup. Regardless of the amount of stress in the cup, mentally and visually empty that cup and begin anew the next day. This is very helpful since we often don't empty our cups and we walk around not knowing whether the next stressful situation we encounter will be the one that causes us to go over the edge or even get sick. This is similar to the saying, "the straw that broke the camel's back." Notice how full your cup tends to get on a daily basis. If it appears to be almost full every day, or even every other day, make a list of your stressors and see what you can eliminate.

We often put ourselves into extremely stressful situations when we are choosing to make change in our lives. I often talk with people who are interested in making four or five major changes in their lives and want to do them all at once; or talk with an athlete who wants to move up two or more skill levels or learn a new skill in a very short time. Both of these not only create a great deal of stress but usually end up in failure. A much more successful approach is to choose one area for change, achieve the transformation, and then chose another. This way you will be building upon success.

12

◆

File: Communication

Communication is the way we relate to each other—between family members, between parents and coaches, athletes and coaches, and supervisors and middle management. Within these relationships are several levels of communication, all of which relate to a willingness to communicate.

We learned about communication from our parents, teachers, and others around us when we were growing up. They became role models for us. We mimicked their style. We witnessed styles ranging from being unwilling to share ourselves with others to being open and honest.

We use words to communicate our feelings, to give and receive feedback. This interaction creates and maintains, or destroys, relationships. The dialogue between two or more people makes up most of our daily communication. The level of comfort within these interactions ranges from being very comfortable to very uncomfortable.

All people speak through two processes or channels: words and feelings. Words create some interference with this process since even the five hundred most commonly used words have approximately 14,000 definitions. We even experience situations where words like "fat chance" and "slim chance" mean the same thing. We speak about one hundred fifty words a minute and think about four times that fast, or at a rate of six hundred words per minute. Making this even more difficult are gender differences. It has been said that men usually speak 12,000 words a day and women about double that, or 25,000. Men tend to speak and hear in facts while women speak and hear through the filter of feelings.

Gaps in communication can and do occur between male coaches and female athletes, female supervisors and male employees, and male board members and female committee members. Being aware of these differences can help avoid the stress, tension, and anxiety that result from miscommunication.

Communication should be redundant, especially that related to learning a new skill or learning new information. When a person is exposed to a new idea, new material, a new way to grip a golf club, or a new way to do a profit and loss statement, repetition is vitally important. If we hear or perform those instructions one time, we will remember approximately 2% of it two weeks later. But if we hear or do the instructions for six consecutive days, we will remember 62% of it two weeks later. That is the power and value of repetition.

The greatest problem with communication is whether what we have communicated (1) has been received and (2) has been received in the manner in which it was intended. Good non-verbal communication skills can help with this problem.

If it is important that your message is heard, see that your message was accurately received and interpreted. For example, messages between boss and supervisor, coach and player, president and board member, should be clear, complete, and direct. They should include feelings clearly stated, based on facts and not opinions only. To be most effective, they should be delivered immediately and not have hidden agendas. Double messages create havoc between communicators. The receiver is confused and the sender is probably using this style of communication because they are afraid to tell the other person something directly.

Another type of confusion occurs when verbal and nonverbal messages are in conflict. Your words may say one thing and your body language another. As much as 75% of our communication is through body language, the non-verbal messages that we send out. Our body language shows that we are shy and uncomfortable or comfortable and expressive. Whichever, we tend to get back what we give out. For example, if we enter a room full of people and one person is alone, looking as if they wished they were just about anywhere else and staring at the floor, we may be uncomfortable approaching them. But, if we see a person who is surrounded by people laughing and talking, we are often more eager to join them.

Just as our body language reveals a lot about us, so does our intonation when we are speaking. Our tone may be overpowering or meek, or in the middle range and assertive. Along with a middle range tone, we should communicate while maintaining eye contact about 50% of the time. We don't need to stare or hold the contact very long; the process itself shows the other person a sense of confidence.

If you have difficulty communicating your thoughts or hearing what others are communicating, check and see where your thoughts are. If you are fearful and doubtful about your ability to communicate, you will share few thoughts or ideas. On the other hand, if you are feeling open and free and not fearful, you can easily and effortlessly communicate your thoughts, and you will feel comfortable with the whole process of communication—verbal and non-verbal.

13

◆

File: Mood

Mood management is the ability to handle the huge array of human emotions in a way that positively impacts our life and performance. These emotions and situations include, but are not limited to, frustration, happiness, anger, success, failure, joy.

You know that the emotional responses in your file cabinet were put there by your experiences up until today. These responses were often mimicked by watching the people around you—parents, teachers, coaches, bosses—as you observed how they expressed their emotions in a variety of situations. As you expressed these acquired responses you were told that your mood responses were acceptable or not acceptable. Or you may have recognized how appropriate or inappropriate they were.

Sometimes the environment itself, the sport or workplace, dictated your responses. A coach may have said it was inappropriate to throw the golf club. Or you observed sport or workplace interactions to see whether your behavior was in line with expectations. Along the way, you have taken the information, modified your inappropriate responses, and fine tuned your appropriate ones.

If you run into situations where you become frustrated, happy, or sad, and your expressions of those feelings have not interfered with moving forward, then you can probably assume that your skills are appropriate. On the other hand, if you find that you have not performed your best, missed a shot, lost a job, lost a point or ball because of your mood responses, then look at some of the following techniques.

You'll primarily need to change your thoughts about certain concepts so you can change your behavior and rule your emotions. Look at those conceptual thoughts that relate to making mistakes, perfectionism, work ethic, and fairness. If athletes get very frustrated at not readily being able to pick up a new skill, they may kick the ice, throw the golf club, or do some other inappropriate behavior response. Changing that will require a change in thinking. An athlete will need to understand that mistakes are a part of learning and he cannot expect to develop a skill in a short amount of time. Or, he may think that, if he works as hard as someone else, he should be able to do what they do. This false thinking creates the feeling that creates the negative behavior.

A simple affirmation to remind you of new ways of thinking will help you immensely. Some suggestions are, "It's okay to make mistakes," or, "My best is all I can do." It is also important to decide that you will express your frustrations later so you will stay focused and concentrate on what you are doing. After the performance or practice session is over, you can figure out how you want to handle your feelings or moods. You may choose to express your feelings to a friend, a fellow employee, your boss, or your coach. Whatever the choice, you are using techniques to handle your emotions in a manner that won't interfere with your practice or performance.

14

◆

File: Fear

Fear is our body's way of telling us that we have left our comfort zone and are attempting something new—we are taking a risk, we're doing something different. We are afraid that maybe we can't learn or do whatever it is that we are trying. We are afraid that we will be a failure.

People need to be re-educated about fear. Fear is a fact of life and can be dealt with that way. We need to pay attention to what we learned about fear (what is in our filing cabinets) and determine what we need to re-learn.

We have many fears—of making mistakes, of not using our time wisely, of making a wrong decision or choice, of being successful, of change, of meeting people, of public speaking, of being an officer of a corporation, of being alone, of not being alone. Some fears are basic and some we create as we try new things. Fear is what causes people to perform in what I call the hope mode—"I hope I can do this" rather than "I have done this hundreds of times before and I can do it that way now."

A future Olympic world-class skater was skating in a competition that was carried by ABC. Due to her skating performance and her draw, for the first time she would be skating with cameras showing her every move. As she came stroking around the corner while warming up, she looked right into the eye of the network camera. Immediately her thoughts were that she couldn't believe that she was skating in a group of elite skaters with national cameras focusing on her. None of her thoughts were on the technical elements of her skating but, rather, on her fears that she could not do what she knew how to do. A high school state level tennis player was excellent in practice, but in competition, would literally freeze, becoming immobile on the court as he was getting ready to serve or receive serve. A swimmer would lose precious seconds while doing a turn at the end of the lane, while an Olympic hopeful in women's hockey was held back from doing her best by thoughts about her unsuccessful past performances.

Fear about their performances, doubts about their technical abilities, concerns about the outcomes and results all keep these athletes from doing their personal best. Their thoughts create feelings of doubt, fear, anxiety, and worry which causes their muscles to tighten up, affecting their bodies ability to do their routines. A normal amount of fear can cause you to get butterflies before a performance, but fear like this can be disabling.

Fear of this type immobilizes you and limits your life and achievements. Ask yourself questions about your fears. "Does the fear mean that I'm not ready to do my presentation, or that I need more training? Maybe I should not attempt this particular jump today. Or, does it mean that I am really prepared but don't have confidence? Am I afraid that I will fail? More importantly, does the fear simply mean that I need to reframe my ideas around fear by adjusting or changing my thoughts?" This re-framing is similar to changing the frame on a picture that needs updating or picking a different color to highlight or match a new décor.

If adjustments are necessary, you can consciously choose to change what is in your files regarding fear. Otherwise, your thoughts regarding fear will keep you from being as successful as you would like to be. Imagine that you are an airplane in route to the next largest city. About halfway there, you take a nose-dive, heading for the ground. As you check yourself out for mechanical problems and fuel, you realize that the problem is weight. You have too much baggage. Immediately, you throw baggage overboard, and you successfully and safely land at your destination.

Your thoughts are like the baggage, they will often keep you from successfully achieving your goals. Most often, it is not that you need to learn more, you simply need to get rid of old beliefs, attitudes, and thoughts that are keeping you from moving forward. One of the greatest of these immobilizing thoughts is fear. If you have fear in your mind, you will have fear in your life and you will behave fearfully. If nothing changes within the contents of your files, nothing changes.

You may not be aware of some of the classic examples where failure is an inherent part of success. You may need to remind yourself that the most outstanding professional basketball teams turnover the ball every three minutes without even shooting it. A highly successful golfer like Ben Hogan said that while playing 18 holes, he usually hit only 2 or 3 balls exactly as he had planned. A graduate student received a C for a paper that he wrote outlining the ideas for a business that became Federal Express; and 3M failed time and time again before becoming the multi-million dollar business it is today.

We need to listen to our internal dialogue and eliminate thoughts that maintain our feelings of fear. Thoughts are our ally and constant companion and, as mentioned before, can be created by us so that we can feel the way we want and we can behave the way we want. We can change our fear-producing thoughts to confidence-producing thoughts—the choice is ours to make.

Fear of success is a difficult concept, but it causes us to subconsciously avoid success at all costs. The underlying fear is that success will change us in some important way that threatens our way of life. For example, a businessman may not want to accept a promotion because it requires a move across the country. An athlete may fear becoming successful because he may not be able to continue his success. These feelings lead to sabotaging himself. In one sense, failure is over and done with while success requires that we work to maintain that level. Sometimes, that pressure can be worse than simply not having succeeded in the first place.

One way to overcome fear is to look at what you are attempting to do and divide that into smaller parts. Looking at the whole task can be overwhelming, while looking at smaller pieces seems more manageable. You can do a little for one day—run 200 more yards, rotate a half turn more, approach one more person.

Another way to overcome fear is to use visualization skills. Imagine the situation and see yourself performing correctly and confidently. If you haven't done this performance well in the past, change the way you perform it by seeing yourself performing in a different way—a more correct way. Your perfect game develops much like an airplane enroute. It is off course almost all the time it is flying (like 90% of the time). It arrives at its destination because the pilot keeps correcting the flight path. See yourself continually correcting your course to embrace success.

Everyone who tries to be successful experiences fear of some sort. But it is the person who has developed skills to deal with fear, who understands that success is a cycle of forward movement and setbacks, who will have the most successful performances.

15

◆

File: Relaxation

Relaxation techniques are skills that allow us to deal with the tension and anxiety that interferes with performance. Athletes and all people have to be able to control their physical movements and their skills in order to do well. Most people can relax when there is little or no pressure or stress. This occurs when you are not the speaker, not the athlete, not the performer. It becomes much more difficult when you feel performance pressure and are nervous.

Almost everyone will be a little bit nervous. It's fair to say that if a person isn't a little bit nervous, they probably don't have the expectation of themselves that they should.

Athletes and performers want to exhibit their skills in a space that has been commonly referred to as the zone. Everyone's zone is a different combination of anxiety and relaxation. As we grow and develop, we should know how we want to feel and how we felt when we experienced peak performance. We should be able to identify that zone and we should be able to mentally put ourselves into that space.

To do this, first identify an example of your finest performance—when you felt confident, you were relaxed, your performance was fluid and flowing. Next, imagine a scale between 1 and 100 and pick a number between 50 and 60. Between 50 and 60 is the ideal mental place for an athlete or performer to be. Higher than 60 usually indicates that a person is trying too hard—they are tense, their muscles are tight, and they are feeling a great deal of pressure. Lower than 50 usually indicates that one is feeling sluggish, not really connected to the task, and has low energy. Let's say that you choose 58. Fifty-eight becomes mentally attached to your best performance. So, from this point on, tell yourself that the best place for you to be mentally, on a scale from 1 to 100 during a performance or practice, is 58.

Prior to this, as you went to practice or perform, your mind went back and remembered the feelings connected with previous performances. We all have performances that were good, performances that were not so good, and ones that were just okay. The problem was that the choice of what to remember was left to chance. Chance may or may not place you in your best mental space. Now, every time you program yourself by attaching 58, you are choosing your best mental space in terms of relaxation, confidence, and performance.

The next step is learning how to activate this mind set. One effective way is to take your right hand and have the pad of your thumb point towards the ceiling. Then take the pads of the first two fingers and put them on the pad of the thumb. This can be done with either hand. You are telling yourself that any time you use that finger-thumb technique, you are focusing yourself into your ideal mental space for performance. This technique is very inconspicuous but extremely effective.

With athletes, an additional method can be used to access their chosen mindset of 58. Hockey players or figure skaters wiping their blades, tennis players twirling their rackets, golfers swinging their clubs, or swimmers shaking their hands before they dive into the water, are all effective movements for creating a brief reminder to focus in their zone. Even just repeating "58" can bring the focus back if the athlete has incorporated that particular technique. Whatever the movement, it should be in the athlete's routine preparation. He is just attaching the concept of an excellent performance state to it.

Athletes and high performance people in the business world need to learn and apply daily relaxation techniques as well. There are various reasons why people need to learn relaxation techniques and their application. Relaxation is a psychological response that creates restfulness. The relaxation response lowers oxygen consumption, respiration rate, heart rate, and muscle tension.

Relaxation skills, as with all of these skills, work best when they have been practiced. Relaxation skills provide the setting for other skill development, particularly the ability to visualize. Peak performances occur when the mind and muscles are relaxed.

Some relaxation techniques include deep breathing, muscle relaxation, imagery, visualization, listening to music, and distracting yourself from tension.

When we are feeling anxious, we breathe with our chests. If we switch to abdominal breathing, we become calmer. You may think you don't need to practice breathing because it's so automatic, but proper breathing is a skill that most of us have forgotten. Practice abdominal breathing twice a day for two weeks. You will know that you are getting better at it if you start feeling lightness, warmth, or a sense of floating. Or, if you become so relaxed that you almost fall asleep, you are getting it.

If your mind wanders when you practice breathing, don't try to ignore any thought that intrudes. It will just come back. Use visualization instead. Imagine yourself taking the thought (going to grocery, returning movies, needing to study for a test) and imagine writing it on a piece of paper. Imagine putting the paper inside a balloon, blowing it up, tying it on a string, and letting it go.

You just don't need that thought right now. After doing this, return to concentrate on your breathing. There will be times when your mind is so filled with thoughts that there is no way to concentrate on breathing, and it would take quite awhile to create that many balloons. When this occurs, it is much better to stop and take care of some of the distracting thoughts.

Listening to music is a relaxation technique but be careful that your choice of music produces the appropriate relaxation response for you. For some people, the desired relaxation response comes from listening to heavy metal, for others that increases tension and stress. Some find classical music relaxing, while others feel it is too slow or not dramatic enough.

Listening to music before a performance can help you find your best level of arousal. Music can fill the "thought cloud" discussed in chapter two and block thoughts that produce pressure and stress. Again, as with listening to music for relaxation purposes, your choice of music is very important. We all have a certain level of tension we try to maintain. If our level gets too low, we look for a way to elevate it; if it's too high, we look for a way to relax.

It is important for you to find your level of readiness—how you want to feel for top performances. Some of you will need to be hyped, others need to be more relaxed. What is important is to find the one that helps you get to the optimal level of arousal for the optimal level of performance. Not having the workable skills to appropriately deal with your tension interferes with performance and lowers confidence.

16

◆

File: Time

We constantly make decisions about how we manage our time and activities. Time management is a skill that successful people in all walks of life have learned to do effectively. On a playing and practice field, in a board-room, or at a business meeting, how to manage and use time wisely is very important. High achievers use their time well.

It is important to establish priorities—where do I need to spend my time to be more productive and more assured of accomplishing my goals. The most time should be spent doing those things that lead to the outcome you want—your goals. Some people find themselves majoring in minor things. They find themselves spending all of their time on little things that will not have any bearing on accomplishing goals. In planning your time, use the 80-20 rule—that 80% of the results will be due to 20% of your activities.

Most of us feel that we never have enough time. We can create time by realistically scheduling those tasks that need to be done. Oftentimes, we assign unrealistic time frames to what needs to be done and find ourselves overwhelmed and under accomplished. We are left wondering where the time has gone and why we have not succeeded in what we were working on. We lose valuable time and motivation when we spend too much time on low priority items. That is not to say that small tasks do not lead to larger accomplishments. But we need to be aware of whether we are spending large amounts of time on lower priority tasks that drain the amount of time and energy left for tasks that will assure us of achieving our goals.

Another time management concern is whether or not we are able to make basic decisions about what we want to do with our time. Our lives are a result of the infinite number of decisions we have made. These decisions have either seemed small and insignificant or incredibility large and important. Regardless, they have all worked together to bring us to where we are today.

If you are happy and feeling productive in relation to your goals and expectations, you are making appropriate decisions about your life. On the other hand, if you find yourself unhappy, frustrated, and feeling stressful or anxious most of the time, that indicates a need to learn how to more effectively make decisions so that you use time wisely.

Several clues indicate that you are making poor choices about time management. One is feeling tired all the time. Another is having periods of time where you are doing very little in relation to your goals. You often need to take time away from your goals to reflect and refresh yourself; but you do not need to remove yourself for large periods of time so that you are overwhelmed by the amount of time it will take to complete the tasks when you return.

In general, when you are not making good decisions about the use of time, you feel overwhelmed and like you never have time for yourself. You are not being as productive working towards your goals as you would like to be and you feel that whatever you are doing is simply not worth it.

When you are making ineffective time management choices, you don't have time for the rest of your life and will find it out of balance. You don't get the proper amount of rest nor have time for leisure activities and important people.

You will also find yourself missing deadlines and time frames that you have set. You might miss the deadline for a presentation, forget to have the agenda prepared for a board meeting on Friday, or not follow your training plan to accomplish a technical skill in your sport.

If you are experiencing some of these situations, here are suggestions for improvement. You can increase your awareness of blocks of time and what can be appropriately accomplished within them; then learn how to match tasks to that unit of time. You can build time into your schedule to handle the unexpected. We will all have interruptions—the ice too soft for practice, traffic, the playing field too wet, the weather not cooperating, or a meeting canceled or changed. You can learn to do two things at once, learn to delegate, get up earlier, change your TV watching habits, or rearrange your days. Perhaps even more importantly, you can learn to say "no."

You can also identify time wasters that interfere with good time management. These time wasters usually fall within one of two categories. In the first category, you spend the majority of your time doing low priority activities rather than doing the high priority activities needed for completion of your goal. In the second category, you spend the majority of your time doing things that have absolutely no relevance to the goal that you are trying to accomplish. For example, you may decide that this is the time to clean out your desk rather than work on a report that is due at the end of the day. Time wasters have you postponing or avoiding activities that need to be done for goal completion. Since some of these activities will involve doing things that you simply don't enjoy, there are several ways you can get through them. You can use positive self-talk. You can reward yourself. You can set a time limit to get the job done quickly, then move to an activity you like.

17

◆

File: Balance

Balance is particularly important—it relates to self-image. If you tend to find yourself doing just one thing in your life, most, if not all, of your identify comes from that one area. This makes it much more difficult when you make mistakes or fail. For instance, in the past too many athletes spent most of their day doing three things—training their skills, working out to get in shape, and sleeping. They repeated this pattern day after day after day. Their entire identity was focused on how well they performed in their sport. It they did well, their training and workouts paid off. If not, they obviously felt that they had not been successful.

Literally, this left them only one area to feel good about and that was how well they slept.

We now believe that when an athlete, or any person, has several areas to connect with and feel good about, there is less pressure to have to succeed in their sport. The most balanced athlete will have the four areas of leisure, work, family, and friends and will be doing activities in each of those areas. That way, if she has a poor performance or makes mistakes in one area, she can still feel successful or good about herself in several or all of the other areas. This means that athletes and other people go to concerts, go to movies, have friends outside of work, and have other interests. This balancing requires a look into your mental file related to time management to make sure you make good choices concerning this balance.

I have often worked with athletes whose entire identity was related to what they did on a particular day in their sport. They literally mimicked the idea that all they were supposed to do was train, train, and train some more. They did not date; they did not go to school, rather correspondence school; they did not develop

124

friends outside their sport; and they did very little with their competitors. As they got older and left their sport, they found themselves ill equipped to handle the other areas of life. They felt awkward dating, they felt awkward engaging people in social situations, and they felt behind in their education and career planning.

This in no way means that athletes or anyone else should have a different focus in their lives than their sports or their goals. We all know that it does require sacrifice and commitment to become so focused that we become very, very skilled and successful. Rather, this suggests that all or the majority of our time should not be spent in one area upsetting the balance of our lives.

Balance is essential as we move through life. All areas of life provide us with experiences for growth and help form how we think, how we feel, and how we act. Having a variety of experiences makes us much more interesting and complete people. We cannot control life, but we can certainly control how we respond to life, business, and sports. By controlling our choices in these areas, we become balanced. That balanced feeling enables us to perform with increased excitement and motivation. When we are balanced, we also experience less pressure and stress. Oftentimes, when we become totally absorbed in our job, our life, our sport, we tend to over analyze everything and feel out of control.

One way to help ensure that your life is balanced emotionally is to imagine that all of your life experiences fall on a scale with a range from 0 to 100. People whose emotional life is out of balance will find themselves soaring and falling from 100 to 0 every time an event occurs. This means that the body is required to move up and down within a 99-point range creating great stress. It is obviously impossible to be balanced with these extremes; when something truly wonderful or sad happens there is little difference between the larger experiences and the everyday. So, by mentally and visually telling yourself that you are going to stay within 30 and 70 when a positive event occurs, other than something extraordinary, you would not experience emotions higher than 70 on your scale. Likewise, if something negative or sad happens, again not extraordinary, emotionally you will not go below 30 on this scale. Now, instead of emotionally dropping and climbing over 99 points when an event occurs, your range would be only 40. This is an excellent way to visually and mentally monitor yourself to find balance and avoid a great deal of stress.

Another way you can create and maintain balance in your life is to make sure that you have enough interactions within the four areas of career/work, leisure, family, and social/friends. Who you are and how you view your interactions in each of those areas is important.

Maintaining a sense of balance within them is equally important. If you assign 25 points to each of these areas, making up a total of 100, you can use that formula for assessing them. For instance, in my life areas, I am a psychologist, an independent business owner, a mother, a friend, and a sister. I have leisure time and work time. If I look at the balance in my life on any given day, I may find that the only thing I achieved was in the career area because that was where I spent most of my time. I give myself 25 points for my career area, but only a few points in the other areas, giving me a balancing score of only 30 or 33 points. We all know that 33 points out of a possible 100 is not good, and from that I could set up feelings of being overwhelmed, out of sorts, and not balanced. On that day, I could feel that I have failed within the other areas of my life. On the other hand, if I make it a habit to assess myself once a week, perhaps on a Sunday evening, I will usually see that during the previous six days I spent a balanced amount of time in each of my priority areas. But, if measuring weekly, my numbers don't appear to be balanced, I need to look at what is occurring and why—some areas are clearly getting more attention and time than others are.

The more we feel good or balanced the more we become addicted to feeling that way; we become intolerant about feeling bad or unbalanced.

18

◆

Putting it all together

The following examples show the application of information contained in the previous files. Each file and its contents, separately and in combination, are vital for successful performance. Remember, as I refer to response settings I am talking about the behavior that is created by the contents of each of these filing cabinets.

In the world of sports....

An elite athlete enters a national level competition with a goal to perform her best, hoping to be one of the top three performers. At the end of the competition, she will have accomplished her goal of doing her best and will be one of the top three performers or she will not have done her best and will not be one of the top three performers.

In the first instance, she accomplishes her goal and becomes not only one of the top three but also the United States champion and will hold the title for a year. She finds herself having to modify many if not all of her response settings. At the very least, three of her response settings are affected, perhaps many more. For example, she is now dealing with a fear of success or a fear of failure—afraid that she could not maintain her position. The experience of winning impacts her self-confidence and her moods. She needs to adjust the picture of herself to reflect that she is now a national champion. Certainly, her ability to adapt comes into play. She has to deal with the many changes that come with being a national champion. Those changes will probably affect how she uses her time. She will have guest performances and other competitions. It is certain that her communication responses have to be adjusted as she finds herself dealing more and more with heightened media attention.

In the second example, she does her best, but ends up in fifth place. Although being fifth in the nation is quite an accomplishment, she may not respond in a positive way to the accomplishment since she is disappointed that, by doing her best, she was only fifth. She, too, will find herself needing to adjust some of her response settings. She could be feeling a fear of failure that impacts her self-image and her mood. If she keeps the same goals for the upcoming year, she will schedule more or fewer practice sessions, more coaching sessions, more workouts, all of which will impact her time management as well as her adaptability responses. She has to determine how to communicate her feelings about the experience this year and express her feelings about new goals.

In the business world...

Due to economic conditions and technology, DGD Company is downsizing. A middle-management executive, who has been with the company for ten years, will be told today whether he will retain or lose his job.

He is notified that he will stay in his position. His self-image is affected as he has almost certainly experienced many negative and positive thoughts about himself while waiting for the announcement. While his initial reaction is one of relief, his fear response will probably shift to a fear of failure from wondering how long it will be before another position is lost due to downsizing, and whether or not it will be his. As the company goals change due to downsizing, he finds it necessary to adjust his individual goals so they mesh appropriately with those of the company. His moods are affected when he moves from the unknown to the known. He most certainly finds himself more relaxed and in a better mood. His communication responses will need to be adjusted as he retained his job within the company.

He is notified that he will not stay in his position. The performance response that needs the most adjustment is his ability to deal with change. Likewise, his self-image is greatly affected. He most likely feels a fear of failure and needs to deal with that response. He most certainly needs to set new goals and communicate those goals to potential employers. He also needs to communicate about the loss of his job. Although his situation has moved from the unknown to the known, his moods reflect sadness and frustration. However, he finds himself in a position where he must present himself confidently as he looks for employment. He will find that the biggest part of his time will now be spent job hunting.

◆

We will experience many situations in life when we need to take a look at the contents of our filing cabinets. We will find ourselves behaving in a manner that we do not like or doesn't seem to fit us. We will want to learn to do something better. We will want to let go of some old tiresome habits. We will want to be more open and expressive. In short, we will want to make changes to do better and make our lives better. When these times occur, my hope is that you will refer to the techniques, tools, and suggestions identified here; develop your High Performance Thinking skills, and become more successful in each and every area of your life. It is an exciting process and one I think you will enjoy. I wish you well!

Acknowledgements

I am grateful to the hundreds of people in all areas of
my life who repeatedly asked me if I had written a
book. You planted the seed.

I am grateful for the inspiration and influence of the
many athletes and coaches I have had the
pleasure of working with.

I am grateful to my editor/book designer for her talent
and steadfast commitment that made the
scheduled completion a reality.

I am grateful to have been blessed with family, friends,
colleagues, corporate executives, and other
independent business owners whose love,
support, and encouragement I could not have
done without.

I am grateful to my son for his love and support.

I am grateful to my parents for the contents of my files.

Gayle A. Davis,
a psychologist, is nationally and internationally
recognized for her seminars on personal growth
and performance in life, sports, and business. In
addition to her clinical practice in Colorado
Springs, Dr. Davis has worked for over twenty
years in sports psychology. She is well respected
for her work with all levels of athletes and coaches,
including World-Class and Olympic contenders.

Contact Information

Dr. Gayle A. Davis
730 West Cheyenne Boulevard
Colorado Springs, CO 80906
Phone: 719-632-5761
Fax: 719-576-2464
E-mail: gadphd@earthlink.net
Web site: www.GayleADavisPhD.com